6610

MICHAEL & TIFFANY ROSS

does

MasterCard™

accept

VISA®

?

and other issues you'll face after graduation

Beacon Hill Press of Kansas City
Kansas City, Missouri

Copyright 2003
by Beacon Hill Press of Kansas City

ISBN 083-412-0259

Printed in the
United States of America

Cover Design: Paul Franitza

10 9 8 7 6 5 4 3 2 1

To Jeanna
Ever since our freshman year of college,
we've stayed in sync. And we've remained close
despite life's ups and downs and all the miles
between us. Thank you, friend.
—Tiffany

To Phillip
"As iron sharpens iron, so one man sharpens another"
(Prov. 27:17). You truly are the "best man."
—Michael

Contents

Part 3: Life-Changing Choices

About the Authors

Michael and Tiffany Ross live in Colorado Springs with their son, Christopher, and two cats. Michael is the editor of *Breakaway* magazine and the author of several books for young people, including *Radically Plugged In.* Tiffany is a former production coordinator for Focus on the Family's films department and is now a full-time mom as well as a student at Fuller Theological Seminary.

Michael and Tiffany love adventure travel. During a recent trip to Africa, they rode motorcycles through Zimbabwe (with a bunch of teens, of course) and then took a safari by boat down the Zambezi River.

Introduction
Finding Your Fit

To man belong the plans of the heart,
*   but from the LORD comes the reply of the tongue.*
All a man's ways seem innocent to him,
*   but motives are weighed by the LORD.*
Commit to the LORD whatever you do,
*   and your plans will succeed.*
The LORD works out everything for his own ends—
*   even the wicked for a day of disaster.*
The LORD detests all the proud of heart.
*   Be sure of this: They will not go unpunished.*
Through love and faithfulness sin is atoned for;
*   through the fear of the LORD a man avoids evil.*
When a man's ways are pleasing to the LORD,
*   he makes even his enemies live at peace with him.*
Better a little with righteousness
*   than much gain with injustice.*
In his heart a man plans his course,
*   but the LORD determines his steps.*
*   —Prov. 16:1-9*

The last year of study is under your belt. A milestone has been reached. A goal has been accomplished. All the struggles of the past years are now forgotten—exams, paper deadlines, disappointment in grades, frustration with teachers. Graduation day is here.

It's time to make plans and move on. It's time to face the future—to find your fit. So what's next? Do you have plans? College? Military? Work? Whatever path you choose, there's one thing you probably dream of more than anything else: *success.*

Solomon shares the keys to a prosperous life—some

golden nuggets of wisdom, so to speak—in Prov. 16:3. First and foremost, make the Lord Jesus number one in your life. That's where success begins. Joseph was carried away into Egypt as a slave and thrown into prison. He succeeded in becoming ruler of Egypt because of one thing and one thing only—his commitment to the Lord.

Set goals for yourself, but as you're doing that, realize that the Lord may have other plans for you. Before his conversion, the apostle Paul wanted to spend his life wiping out Christianity. But God's plan was for Paul to be His greatest missionary:

> You have heard of my previous way of life in Judaism, how intensely I persecuted the church of God and tried to destroy it. I was advancing in Judaism beyond many Jews of my own age and was extremely zealous for the traditions of my fathers. But . . . God . . . set me apart from birth and called me by his grace (and) was pleased to reveal his Son in me so that I might preach him among the Gentiles *(Gal. 1:13-16)*.

Always fit yourself into what God wants for you rather than trying to fit God into what you want for yourself.

And remember to do what is kind, just, and loving—even if the money's not as good. "Better a little with righteousness than much gain with injustice" (Prov. 16:8).

Consider the rich man and Lazarus in Luke 16:19-31. The rich man had unbelievable wealth but kept it selfishly for himself and ended up on the wrong side of the tracks. True success reaches beyond the grave into eternity.

"We must all appear before the judgment seat of Christ, that each one may receive what is due him for the things done while in the body, whether good or bad" (2 Cor. 5:10). When your life on earth is over, the question will be "How did you spend the life Jesus gave you?"

Introduction

This book will help you set some life goals with that essential question in mind. In addition to a lot of practical advice about life on your own, we'll show you how to make Matt. 25:21 your own so that one day you'll hear Jesus say, "Well done."

Part 1

Launching Your Dreams

Plot a Course

The LORD is near to all who call on him,
to all who call on him in truth.
He fulfills the desires of those who fear him;
he hears their cry and saves them.
—Ps. 145:18-19

God created you with abilities and talents to serve Him in very specific and significant ways. We're all part of the Body of Christ—the Church—that Paul tells us about in 1 Cor. 12:12-31. And though there are many members of the Body, there is still one Body, one cause—one Creator we serve. Paul explained, "The body is a unit, though it is made up of many parts; and though all its parts are many, they form one body. So it is with Christ. . . . Now you are the body of Christ, and each one of you is a part of it" (1 Cor. 12:12, 27).

While God bestows an amazing array of gifts upon His creation, He has chosen each member to make a unique contribution to the Body. In other words, the Body *needs* each member, and each member *needs* the Body. And each member is called to be loyal to his or her Head, the Master, to fulfill His purpose for his or her life, to perform the functions that keep the body vibrantly alive and in step with the Head, the living Head, our Lord Jesus Christ.

When it comes to professions and pursuits, what makes some people successful while others flounder? The key is to find your unique place in this world—and ultimately, true fulfillment—if you *fit yourself into what God wants for you rather than trying to fit God into what you want for yourself.*

Does MasterCard Accept VISA?

Successful people have found their place within the Body. They don't waste their God-given talent on pursuits that counter God's will. Guided by a clear personal vision of what Christ wants them to accomplish in life, they possess an accurate and precise picture of the work that expresses them best. They have identified their talents and are using them. As a result, these individuals experience profound and lasting benefits: reduced stress, more balance, a more productive career, and a more satisfying life.

Are these your desires as well? If so, plot a course for your life by taking the following steps.

Step 1: Focus your vision.

You need to ask yourself two critical questions: *How do I find my place within the Body? How do I pick a profession that's in tune with God's will for my life?*

A close relationship with Jesus is the foundation. Is God directing your steps? If so, Prov. 16:3 promises that you're on the right track: "Commit to the LORD whatever you do, and your plans will succeed." But your plans have no strength if they're not from God.

The Holy Spirit deals with each human being in a personal and intimate way, convicting, directing, and influencing us. You can walk in His presence minute by minute. But you have to do your part and stay connected daily through quiet times, prayer, and Bible reading.

Jesus communicates with you in a variety of ways. The Lord answers your questions and guides your steps through Scripture, prayer, circumstances, and even the counsel of others in your life. It's good to consult with wise Christian people and to seriously consider their counsel as you plot your course.

Peace and a sense of confidence are the signs of spiritual awareness. Peace is often a good indication that you're on the right track. And as you grow closer and closer to Christ, your instincts will become more sensitive to His influence. Your mind and spirit will become more in tune to God, and you'll begin to hear Him more clearly, just as with any other good friend.

Step 2: Dare to dream.

We're not talking about the kind of dreaming that's a result of mouth-wide-open-snoring-on-the-pillow activity. Do some serious soul-searching and think about your interests, desires, and the kind of career that genuinely interests you. And while you're at it—

• **Consider the gifts and talents God has given you.** Ask God to reveal what His "good, pleasing, and perfect will" for your life looks like (Rom. 12:2).

• **Share your dreams.** Talk with your parents and/or with an adult you trust who can possibly be your mentor. Let people know about your dreams and aspirations. Their input will be valuable in finding the life pursuit that will best shape the person inside you.

Step 3: Pinpoint your passion.

Let's zero in on your abilities. Respond to the following six critical statements:

I'm often described as (circle only sets of words and phrases):

> Mechanically minded/technical
> Inventive/a problem-solver
> Creative/artistic
> An outdoor enthusiast/adventurous
> Athletic/competitive
> Scientific/mathematical
> Investigative/a fact-finder
> Legal-minded/detail-oriented
> A people person/a communicator
> A planner/an organizer

Places I prefer to work include

> Urban locations/suburban locations/remote locations

Does MasterCard Accept VISA?

Indoors/outdoors/both indoors and outdoors

These geographic locations (list your top three choices):

1.

2.

3.

These specific organizations (list your top three choices):

1.

2.

3.

I most enjoy a working environment that's described as (circle all that apply):

Corporate

Busy and public

Filled with new challenges every day

Stressful, even chaotic

Routine

Quiet and private

Highly creative

Orderly and structured

Somewhat dangerous

Competitive

Materials I enjoy working with include:

Tasks I enjoy most:

Fields of knowledge that interest me include (write your top five choices):

1.
2.
3.
4.
5.

Step 4: Set some goals.

A goal is the end toward which you direct your effort. Similar to scoring a goal in sports, you'll strive to attain them and will find joy in achieving them. And as soon as you reach one goal, you can't wait to reach the next one. Don't be afraid to set goals for your life.

Remember these three things about a life goal: It's concrete, it's measurable, and it's attainable.

A concrete goal is one you can put into words. A vague desire to "be a good Christian" is not very concrete. But "Join InterVarsity Christian Fellowship my freshman year" is a solid goal. Goals are most concrete when written down.

A measurable goal is one that allows you to see progress. "Know the Bible from cover to cover" is tough to measure. But "Read the New Testament this summer" allows you to mark your progress with that little ribbon-dealie in your Bible.

An attainable goal is one that can reasonably be completed. "Lead the world to Christ" is both concrete and measurable but hardly attainable. "Introduce three people to Jesus before I graduate from college" is a goal that meets all three criteria.

Step 5: Seek God and pray

Prayer is a key step in setting your goals and dreams in motion. Take an afternoon, a weekend, an hour a day for a month—whatever you need—and pray. Above all, listen to God. Focus on His voice and direction for your life.

Next, begin writing some concrete, measurable, attainable goals for your life. Write them in rough form and then type them out. You'll want a clean copy to review and rehash on occasion in the future. Setting life goals shouldn't be a one-time affair.

Ivory Tower Survival Tips

Blessed is the man who finds wisdom, the man who gains understanding, for she is more profitable than silver and yields better returns than gold.
—Prov. 3:13-14

It's one of life's mile markers, a Kodak moment. The day Mom and Dad leave you standing on the curb at college will be etched in your brain forever. Suddenly reality hits. You're on the brink of a whole new life in a whole new place. It will be exciting and terrifying. In some ways it will be a lot like starting high school, just a little more intense and probably a lot farther from home.

Let's take a peek at what college is like through the eyes of a college freshman.

Freshman Diaries

August 15—one week before leaving for college

I'm so overwhelmed and excited and scared. I've waited so long for the day I leave for college—I can't believe it's one week away. Even though I've been getting ready all summer (actually all my life), I still have so much to do. It'll be OK though—Mom is doing most of it. She bought one of those small refrigerators from my uncle for my dorm room. It's used, but it works. I hope she fills it up with food I like when they help me move in—not any of that "healthy" stuff.

I've been going out every night lately with my friends. Tracey, Michael, Toby, and Cindy are all going to school about an hour away from here. They'll get to come home every weekend. I'm excited about being out on my own, and I don't understand why anyone would want to come home from college every weekend. Other than me, Rick and Tina are the only ones of my friends going to school out of state. I can't wait to get together with everybody at Christmas to tell all our stories.

I'd better go now. It's 1:30 A.M., and I'm supposed to get up in the morning and mow the lawn. WOW—I'm going to be so glad when I don't have to worry about doing chores. One more week. One more week.

September 6—Week One of college

I've been so busy that I haven't even had time to journal.

This place is great. They sure do have a lot of rules, though. Not just rules from the school, but other kinds of rules. The whole social structure is different. Nobody seems to be impressed that I lettered in three sports and maintained a 3.8 GPA in high school. It's like I'm starting over. I look around and realize that almost everybody here did well in high school. Everybody is so segmented here. The first question out of everyone's mouth is, "So what's your major?" I'm in my first semester—I have no idea what my major is.

My mattress is lumpy, and the food is really, really bad. I mostly just eat cereal every meal. I love living in the dorm. My roommate's cool and knows a lot of people. We have two or three new people over every night.

I haven't really gotten into my classes yet. On the first day of each class, they handed out a really detailed syllabus. I think they just do that to intimidate the freshmen. There's no way we are actually going to get that much stuff done in one semester.

September 27—Week Four

I'm so tired. This week I have to turn in two five-page papers, finish reading *Lord of the Flies,* visit three or four art galleries, and take a test in my Biology 101 class. This is ridiculous! How am I supposed to get all of this done?

I average only about four hours of sleep a night. There are so many cool people on my floor. We've formed kind of a group. We live together, eat together, go to campus parties together, and then stay up half the night just telling stories and laughing. Last Tuesday we skipped all of our classes and went to see three movies back to back. I've never done that before.

I still haven't figured out which church to go to. I haven't even gone for the last two weeks. I could just go with my friend Susan from down the hall, but her church is so boring.

I have to go now—my roommate just walked in with about 10 people. I guess they're going to watch some movies and do whatever else they do. Maybe I'll just go down the hall and find someone else's room to crash in.

October 23—Week Seven

I am so upset! I can't believe this is happening. I just got a paper back in English, and I got a D minus. I've never gotten that low a grade before. Plus—he told me that I should go somewhere and learn how to write before I ever attempt to write at the college level again. I can't believe he's so mean. Just because he wrote a book, he thinks he's better than everybody else. It's too late in the semester to drop this class. I don't know what to do.

I was supposed to go on a date last night. That didn't happen. Cancelled because of a head cold. I'm so sure!

I have so much to do—if I stayed up for the next three days I wouldn't get it all done. How in the world are other people getting all of this stuff done? My room is so dirty I can't even find my books half the time. I wish I had my own computer. I keep forgetting to sign up for the computer bay in the library. Every time I show up, they're already booked for the rest of the day. I had to pay this guy $25 to type a five-page paper for me last week. I don't have $25 to throw away, and I can't keep calling home for money. I need to get a job, but I don't have time for a job!

I'm so hungry. But I'm broke, so I guess I'll go to the cafeteria and eat some more cereal—yuck.

Well, it's time to go. Here comes my roommate with some more weird friends. Do these people even go to our school? Last week I asked if we could have at least a couple of nights a week with no visitors, and all I got was a strange look and a laugh. I guess we should have settled it at the first of the semester when it started.

November 24—Week Twelve

Well, I think I've found a church to go to. I visited one yesterday that I really liked, but I'm not really sure what they believe in. I snagged some of their literature as I left, so I guess I should read it before next weekend so I can figure out if I should go back.

I finally figured it out! I talked to one of the librarians, and she told me how to sign up for a computer weeks in advance. It's great. I've been in there three times this week, and I'm getting so much done. Just in time too! My parents would blow a fuse if they saw how bad my grades were after my midterms. If I'm not careful, they may not send me back next year.

My little group of friends has dwindled. There are only about three of us now—me, Joey, and Susan. Greg got kicked out for drinking too much, and Gina decided that college wasn't a good fit for her and left—even before the first semester was over. Julie decided to take a job at home; I think she just wants to go home so she can get married. It's OK, though. Joey and Susan seem to be the solid ones anyway. I've been spending so many hours in the library lately I really don't have much extra time anyway.

I'd better go to bed now—I have a huge exam at 8 o'clock. Why do they schedule classes so early in the morning?

December 14—Week Fifteen

My first semester is over. I just took my last final! I didn't do so great this semester, but I'm optimistic for next semester. I think I'm getting the hang of this. I'm still going to have a lot of explaining to do when my parents see my GPA. I hope they understand that adjusting to college has been way hard for me.

Oh, yeah—I almost forgot. My roommate is moving out! Yea! Since they don't let freshmen have single rooms, I'm sure I'll have a new roommate next semester. That's OK—I already have a list of topics to discuss right up front.

Other good news—I got a job on campus. Next semester I'll be answering phones four nights a week in the phone room. It's boring, but they say you can study between phone calls. I really need the extra money—I'm so sick of cereal.

A Few Keys to College Success

List your expectations. What is my GPA goal for the first semester? How many new friends do I expect to make? Will I spend my money on food or movies?

Befriend an upperclassman. Ask him or her how things work around your campus, such as, Where is the best place to study? How do you sign up for a computer or study room at the library? Is there a fun (and safe) place to hang out and meet people? Which professors does he or she recommend?

Balance your social life. Above all, don't let the fun times collide with your academic demands. Keep in mind why you went to college.

Do laundry. It's cheaper than buying new underwear every time you run out. Also remember to use dryer sheets.

Use your textbooks. Don't try to keep them in good shape with the hopes of selling them back at the end of the semester. Usually you get only a small portion (if any) of the cost back.

Find ways to make some extra cash. For example,

Does MasterCard Accept VISA?

consider getting a job on campus. It may not pay as much as other employment, but the commute is very convenient! Also, inquire about openings in specific departments that spark your interest. The experience may help you choose your major.

Don't be afraid to ask questions. Hey—it's probably obvious that you're a freshman, so cut the cool act. The more quickly you learn the ropes, the sooner you can settle into a routine.

Take notes in every class—even if it doesn't seem important at the time. Keep a separate notebook for each class.

Plug into a local church. While friends may get you pointed in the right direction, you may have to launch a search by yourself. After all, your worship preferences may be different from theirs. Bottom line: Pray about this one a lot—it's the only way you'll end up in the church God wants you to attend. (See chapter 10 for more on this important topic.)

Connect with your new roommate. This is a biggie! Within the first week of school, make a list of things to discuss with your new roommate—and don't delay in going over them together. Here are some suggestions of what to talk about:

What time do you go to bed?

How often do you have guests over?

Are we going to share food, or should we label each item?

What kind of music do you like? Do you like it loud?

Make a list (with dates) of who will clean the bathroom each week.

Do you like to share clothes, music, movies, and so on?

Do you plan to study in the room or somewhere else?

How do you feel about drinking and smoking?

3

Getting into the 9-to-5 Routine

Whatever you do, work at it with all your heart,
as working for the Lord, not for men, since you know that
you will receive an inheritance from the Lord as a reward.
It is the Lord Christ you are serving.
—Col. 3:23-24

With high school screeching to a halt and the endless possibilities of adulthood ahead, we know what you're thinking: *I'm tired of having nothing but lint balls and gum wrappers in my pockets. I'm ready for some serious cash—BUT HOW CAN I GET IT?*

The answer, of course, is to get a job!

But nearly everyone will tell you that it's a "job jungle" out there, and the Sunday classifieds look as if they're written in secret code. And the age-old question: how do you get work experience when most good jobs require you to have experience?

Suddenly you feel the panic of unemployment pressing in, and your confidence begins to wane. Launching out on your own is scarier than you thought! You may be feeling that it would have been easier just to stay in high school forever.

Don't let your self-esteem suffer. While it's true that your employment options are somewhat limited right out of high school, entering the workforce isn't impossible. Whether you're seeking employment to help pay for college or you've opted to plunge head-first into the 9-to-5 routine, the following pages can help you through the three essential steps of your job search.

Step One: Pinpoint Your Pursuit

There's a big difference between working for a paycheck and working with a purpose. While having a positive attitude is an important factor here, the key ingredients are (1) discovering your talents and (2) using your talents to their fullest.

God wired each of us with raw talent—the ability to be remarkable at something. But for way too many people, "interests" and "work" are two entirely separate subjects. You can vow to be different. Examine carefully what you're drawn to in life—the pursuits that fascinate you. Then go for your dreams!

Identify your interests. Do you enjoy being outdoors? Maybe landscaping or being a lifeguard is for you. Are you athletic? Look for a job at a sporting goods store. Do you drink a lot of cola or coffee? Think about working at a place that sells a good cup of joe, such as Starbuck's, or a company that distributes soft drinks.

"Use your imagination as you think about employment possibilities," says the manager of human resources at Coca-Cola in Atlanta. "Of course, we hire people who enjoy our products."

Assess your skills. Next to interest comes ability. "If you play team sports, I'm definitely interested in hiring you," says Tim, a manager at a sporting goods shop in Bellevue, Washington. "You learn about equipment as you play. Equipment knowledge is the hard part; the selling part you can learn here."

Assess your experience. Do you have work experience? This is important to potential employers, because it shows that you're responsible. Every job gives you skills for another job.

"Just get your foot in the door," says John, a manager

at Kroger Foods in Brentwood, Tennessee. "And once you get a job, stick with it for a while. This shows that you're responsible."

Don't just blend in with the masses and settle for a paycheck. Stand out in the crowd, and pinpoint the kind of job that gives you meaning and purpose—then go for it.

Even if you know what you want, you may not be sure how to track down your ideal job. This calls for some creativity, some outside-the-box thinking. In addition to combing the classified ads, take some time to network. Make your dreams known to Aunt Edna and your parents' friends. In fact, friends who already have jobs are a great resource, and so are your school's career counselors. Also, call local businesses to see if they're hiring, and ask politely to speak with a manager.

Step Two: Write Your Résumé

In high school you probably took a class that taught you how to write a résumé that lists your skills and previous work experience. "It's what gets you in the door," says Trish, director of Microsoft's summer internship program, which hires technically minded people (including recent high school graduates). "The résumé says a lot."

Not only does your résumé help a potential employer see the skills you can offer the company, but the exercise of putting together a résumé gives you the opportunity to think and reflect about your abilities and how they could apply to the job you want. Thinking these things through will help you when speaking to a potential employer.

So what's important to include in a résumé, and what should you leave out? Here's what we suggest.

References: an important selling point. Mom, Dad, and Aunt Edna won't carry much pull as references—they would each be considered pretty biased. But a teacher, a school counselor, a previous employer, even your pastor—these are prime references.

Does MasterCard Accept VISA?

Future bosses are seeking credible individuals who can help them answer two key questions about you: (1) Are you a person of integrity? (2) Can you succeed in this position?

Most places require two or three references. Be sure to include addresses and phone numbers on your résumé.

What to leave off your résumé. Good résumés are persuasive and concise. Each entry should seek to convince potential employers that you are the candidate they should hire. With this in mind, here's what you should omit in order to keep your résumé well focused:

Salary requirement. Why price yourself out of a job or show that you're a bargain?

Reason for leaving a past job. It's best to provide this information during an interview.

Hobbies and outside interests. Above all, avoid listing dangerous or time-consuming activities. The exceptions, of course, are hobbies and outside interests that relate to the profession you're seeking or that reflect personal traits that a potential employer may want.

Sample Résumé

Joe Graduate–123 Mountain Dew Lane, High Potential, CO 00000. 111-234-5566

Goal: Securing a public relations position that involves working with the media, photography, coordinating daily schedules, and planning events.

Work Experience

Youth Pastor Assistant–Victory Community Church. Part-time employment since June 2002. Led worship, planned retreats, coordinated snack schedules, reported to Board of Elders.

Junior Reporter, **KHOPE Radio**—Summers of 1999, 2000, 2001, and 2002. Assisted reporters, helped plan and schedule stories, wrote news copy.

Photography Service—Self-employed since 1997. Provide photography services for more than 20 customers.

Skills

Strong planning and organizing skills. Fast, efficient. Creative. A people person. Solid writing and editing skills. Excellent communicator.

School/Extracurricular

Graduate, Greenwood High School (GPA 3.20)

Student Body President, Greenwood High School

Newspaper Editor, *Greenwood High School Gazette*

Photography Club, Greenwood High School

References:

Youth Pastor, Victory Community Church, 1111 Narrow Road, High Potential, CO 00001. 111-567-8899

N. V. Peale, Principal, Greenwood High School, 222 Education Way, High Potential, CO 00002. 111-568-9900

John Testimony, KHOPE News Director, 33 Televangelist Highway, High Potential, CO 00003. 111-569-HOPE

Step Three: Land a Face-to-Face Interview

Fortunately, you didn't waste your high school years majoring in popularity and parties. You spent your time on more worthwhile pursuits: getting good grades, focusing your photography skills, getting your feet wet volunteering in a local newsroom, being mentored by your youth pastor.

Then one day, just a few months after graduation, you receive a call from a representative of High Potential Employment Agency (the place where you dropped off your résumé). He wants to meet you for an interview.

"Help!" you say, panicking. "I don't know anything about interviews. All I know is photography and writing."

Relax. You're several steps ahead of most high school graduates. In fact, you're just a few more steps away from landing a job.

Put your best face forward. Like it or not, appearance counts. Put on your Sunday best, and give that hair a decent style. "If you want to work in my restaurant, you have to look professional," says Bob, owner of a McDonald's in Woodland Park, Colorado. "First impressions are important to me, because that's the first thing the customer sees."

Have a positive personality. Don't be afraid to smile big and show off those awesome pearly whites! Your personality is your biggest selling point. "I look for people who are outgoing," says Jay, manager at a T.G.I. Friday's restaurant in Tacoma, Washington. "We're out in the public, and you're constantly onstage. You're expected to perform, to look good, to be courteous."

Glenn, a manager of a Pasadena, California, bookstore, agrees. "You need to have some confidence in what you can do," he says. "If you don't think you can get the job, I'm not going to give it to you.

"Even so," he adds, "some of the best employees I've had were really, really shy. But once they got some self-confidence, they became the best customer relations people that I've ever had."

Be a person of integrity. A person's integrity—or lack of it—may be the strongest factor in hiring decisions. T.G.I. Friday's has a checklist on integrity that evaluates the applicant's honesty, warmth, values, and credibility.

"I look for honesty in everybody I hire," Jay, the manager, says. "If you've been fired from a job, tell me. Above all, never, never lie during an interview."

Don't forget to follow up. Once you've made that fabulous first impression, it's time to check back. "It's really important," says Tim, a sporting goods shop manager. "Just call in a week or so and say, 'Hello. This is Joe Graduate. I interviewed with you last week, and I want to follow up on that.' It shows you're interested and willing to work."

Know what you want, submit a professional résumé, look professional, and have a confident attitude during your interview. If you take these important steps during your employment search, it won't be long before you hear these incredible words: "Congratulations—you got the job!"

Six ways to get your foot in the door. Here are some good ways to get that interview:

1. Use a mature, "professional" voice when you call on the phone.

2. If you know someone who already works at the business, ask him or her to recommend you. Mention his or her name when you speak to the employer.

3. Research the business before the interview. Then mention what you learned: "I noticed that at your Topeka store . . ."

4. Let the employer know you're willing to adjust your schedule to fit the work schedule instead of vice versa.

5. Offer to work a day for free to give the employer a chance to judge your abilities.

6. If no long-term position is available, suggest odd jobs you could do for the business.

Portions of this chapter are adapted from Katherine Bond, "Journey Through the Job Jungle," Breakaway, June 1996, and are used with permission of the magazine's publisher, Focus on the Family.

4

Military Life
Choose Your Uniform

*Put on the full armor of God, so that when the day of evil comes,
you may be able to stand your ground, and after you have done
everything, to stand.*
—Eph. 6:13

The familiar aroma of coffee and bacon. The constant clink of mugs and plates and mismatched silverware being scooped up by overworked waitresses. The sudden bolts of laughter from the regulars—usually stubble-faced old-timers—amusing themselves with endless war tales.

Rich smiled as he glanced around the tiny diner, his favorite hometown hangout. He couldn't imagine a better place to be on a Saturday morning. The 17-year-old especially enjoyed spending time with his dad. Breakfast at this greasy spoon was a tradition.

Every Saturday since Rich could remember, his father roused him out of bed and whisked him off to a gut-busting plate of biscuits and gravy. And each Saturday was repeated a thousand times during his childhood: father and son sliding into the same booth, ordering the same food, and socializing with the same stubble-faced men—mostly friends of Rich's dad.

After the usual greetings were exchanged, the conversation would invariably move from the weather ("Hear about the snowstorm that's headed this way?") to the latest political race ("I think our guy has a good chance of winning this go-around") and on to what Rich found most interesting—those amazing war stories.

Not only did Rich learn what his dad was like during his fit-and-trim army days (which he probably would never have otherwise discovered), he also got an earful about military life, not to mention detailed accounts of experiences that profoundly shaped past generations.

Rich was mesmerized by the stories he heard—tales of incredible army invasions, a navy man's adventures on the high seas, and air force missions that were nearly foiled by the enemy. Most of the conversations fell into one of two categories: "faith under fire" and "how I survived some impossible circumstances." (Hey, Indiana Jones—eat your heart out!)

The old guys would shake their heads and laugh, admitting that it took more than one blunder before their thick skulls comprehended a valuable lesson: Breaking the rules, they recalled, always involves consequences. They agreed that their life lessons had always come the hard way.

In the end, the tone inevitably grew serious, and a few eyes got misty. The men would turn the conversation to patriotism and honor and how proud they were to serve their country.

Rich sat listening, glued to every word.

Choosing a Life of Service

Those Saturday morning excursions to the diner left Rich with a positive impression of the armed forces. So it came as no surprise to his father when Rich expressed an interest in a military career. Eventually he took the plunge. A few months after his college graduation, he enlisted in the army, signing on the dotted line.

By no means did the decision come lightly. He spent the entire four years of college wrestling with the thought. Above all, he prayed and prayed and prayed.

Rich also sought some serious counsel from his father,

who always responded with "Kid, it's up to you, so be sure this is what you really want. You—and only you—will have to fulfill the commitment."

Rich took the ASVAB (Armed Services Vocational Aptitude Battery), which is the entrance exam for all enlisted military personnel. He survived the poking and prodding of his physical examination, and he spent several hours researching the job specialties offered by each branch. He also thought about how much money he could receive for graduate school and even gave some thought to applying to Officer's Candidate School, since completing his college education had given him this option.

Finally, Rich made the decision to enlist in the army. No doubt he was scared and excited at the same time. But he survived basic training as well as Advanced Individual Training and soon found himself driving around in a Hummer (high-mobility, multi-purpose wheeled vehicle) on a nighttime mission. Army life wasn't easy, but for Rich it was definitely worth it.

To this day, Rich strongly believes that his success in the military was based on waiting for God's timing. Tapping into God through prayer enabled him to make the right decision at the right time.

Today Rich often catches himself telling his own army stories—shaking his head and laughing at all the life lessons he has learned.

Be All That You Can Be: Prepare Now!

Interested in joining a branch of the military? Unsure if it's the right fit for you? Here's what we suggest you do:

• **Pray.** God's timing is often quite different from yours. If you want to pursue His will, follow His guidance. And the only way to get a clue about God's will is by being in communication with Him—so pray!

• **Do your homework.** Research each military branch. Which one feels right to you? Which one offers the Military Occupation Specialty you would like to pursue? Is active duty or reserve duty right for you? How long are you willing to commit to military life? What are the entrance requirements (both physical and academic)? Do you want to go to Jump School? How much college money will you qualify for?

• **Interview veterans.** Don't just listen to television commercials or your local recruiter. Learn what those who have actually lived the life have to say about it. Each person's experience will be different, and you'll likely hear a large array of comments ranging from "I hated it" to "It was the best thing I ever did." Ask them all why they feel as they do. Get details.

• **Start exercising.** If you join, being fit will only help you. If you don't, being in shape is still a plus. Push-ups, sit-ups, and a lot of running will cover the basics. Also, exercise will help you meet the required weight restrictions for enlistment.

• **Catch the significance.** Trust us: military life is all-encompassing. It's a 24/7 job—truly a lifestyle. If you go for it, be ready to go all the way, at least until you've fulfilled your contract. You'll have a miserable experience if you try to just get by. We're convinced that the intensity of this lifestyle is the reason why so many people vividly remember their military experience for many, many years.

Part 2

Stuff Your Mother Never Taught You

5

There's No Turning Back

*When I was a child, I talked like a child, I thought like a child,
I reasoned like a child. When I became a man,
I put childish ways behind me.*
—1 Cor. 13:11

As I (Tiffany) drove through Pineville, the West Virginia town where I grew up, I couldn't wait to pull up in my parents' driveway and burst through the front door. It had been four months since I had left for college—which, frankly, was nothing short of a whirlwind experience.

Like many other students, I went straight from high school graduation into an extremely busy summer of preparing for college, packing, and tying up a zillion last-minute details. The next thing I knew—boom! I was standing on a college campus.

So getting back to familiar territory was exactly what I needed. Besides, I couldn't wait to fill everyone in on my new life as a college freshman. I had a lot to talk about: everything from my new friends, demanding classes, and dorm life to the less-than-satisfactory cafeteria food. I felt as if I were coming home from an extra-long, extra-intense summer camp.

As I drove through the town and the windy countryside, I daydreamed about my mom's cooking. I couldn't wait to collapse onto the cozy couch in our TV room, savor the smell of clean laundry, visit my hometown friends —even run a few errands to the grocery store for Mom and Dad.

Does MasterCard Accept VISA?

OK, so those were my expectations. But keep in mind an important fact of adult life: Expectations and reality are sometimes very different, especially when it comes to visiting parents and family. So how I envisioned my visit wasn't exactly the way things turned out.

Oh, sure—my family and house all appeared to be exactly the same. But a day or so into my visit, I began to experience many strange emotions. At first I thought I was getting sick or that perhaps I was just really worn out. After much rest and more than a few aspirins, the feeling only seemed to worsen. I felt removed from my surroundings—sort of as if I were out of place in my own house. This was a new and unfamiliar experience for me. Now don't get me wrong. Overall, my visit home was great. I got a lot of attention, and my family spent endless hours listening to my stories. Before I knew it, I was packing up my little Toyota and heading back to school. But the strange feeling stayed with me the whole time.

It's Called Growing Up!

Today, several years later, I understand what was going on. It can be summed up by one phrase: "You can't go home again." Sure, you can visit your family, stay in your old bedroom, and attend the same church. Everything may look exactly the way it was when you lived there. But here's the deal: you've changed. You've done some growing up, and now you have your own life, complete with a new address, new educational demands, and maybe even a new job. It's as if you're floating between two different worlds.

There's no reason to be alarmed or feel overwhelmed. This change in your life is totally normal. Every adult who doesn't still live with his or her parents has gone through this same process in one way or another.

Accepting Change

This is a very exciting time for you, because the possibilities are endless. You've reached a turning point—a new phase of your life in which you must figure out who you are as an adult, what you want to pursue, and how you want to live your life.

The fact is, independence comes with a huge load of responsibility—there's simply no way around it. It's up to you to skip the late movie to study for an exam. It's up to you to brush your teeth and to clean your clothes. It's up to you to keep gas in your car. Get the point? If you make wise decisions, you'll reap the benefits. If you make unwise decisions, you'll also reap the benefits. It's up to you.

6

When Loneliness Strikes

I will not leave you as orphans; I will come to you.
—John 14:18

Rachel flipped off the monitor and sighed in relief. She had spent the last week putting the final touches on her term paper titled "Internet Commerce," and it was finally completed. Her world had revolved around her assignment: endless hours in the library, surfing the Internet, reading books, thumbing through magazines for the latest stats. She had even had nightmares about her paper and had been consumed by data and deadlines.

Now Rachel was ready to celebrate and have some fun. She was determined to get as far away from anything remotely connected with Internet commerce as she could.

She excitedly ran down her list of close friends, even some not-so-close friends, punching the numbers into her cell phone, but all she got was voice mail and answering machines. *Where is everybody? This campus is like a morgue!*

Rachel's mood took a nosedive. Suddenly it hit her. Everybody else had already made their weekend plans while she was chin deep in her term paper. She was facing a couple of days pretty much on her own.

Rachel glanced across her room and spotted her term paper setting on her desk. The words *INTERNET COMMERCE* seemed to jump right off the pages.

Does MasterCard Accept VISA?

"Now what? It's time to party, and I'm sitting here alone with my paper!"

Rachel slumped back on her bed, spiraling into self-pity. Celebration was forgotten.

Chicken Soup for the Blahs

Loneliness: it strikes at the strangest times. One minute you're on top of the world; then, in the next second, you're alone in a pit. Everybody's been there and has experienced the disappointment and discouragement. At times like this, you just have to wonder, *Where are my friends when I need them? How could I have avoided this?*

Some people, maybe even you, go straight to an anti-loneliness vow: "I promise I'll never let this happen again."

When you find yourself face-to-face with loneliness, don't get mired down in negative emotions. Try to keep it in perspective, and evaluate your situation.

Understand your emotions. Your feelings rise and fall like a wild ride on a roller coaster. When you're lonely and depressed, when everything seems to be going wrong and life doesn't seem to be worth living, you need to ride it out. It may not feel very good for a while, but if you ride out these emotions, you'll discover that your circumstances will change tomorrow. Your world will seem much better. Happiness will return, and the depression will disappear.

Ask yourself these questions:
- Why do I feel so lonely? Am I homesick? Am I anxious about something or just too tired?
- How can I come to feel that I am enough and find wholeness in the fact that I'm God's creation? How can I begin to secure in my identity in Christ—even if that means being alone from time to time?
- What steps can I take to work through this loneliness?
- Could this be depression? Do I need professional help to work through these emotions?

Allow yourself to cry. Don't be embarrassed by those

raw, uncomfortable feelings tangled up inside you. Go ahead and let the tears flow. Jesus understands, and He'll be right there with you.

C. S. Lewis says in one of his writings, *Letters of C. S. Lewis,* "The thing is to rely only on God. The time will come when you will regard all this misery as a small price to pay for having been brought to that dependence. Meanwhile (don't I know) the trouble is that relying on God has to begin all over again every day as if nothing had yet been done" (220).

Connect with Christ. Pray. Pour out your heart, and tell Jesus everything you're feeling—everything! *I feel alone . . . angry . . . jealous . . . scared.* Don't worry—nothing you say will shock the Lord or cause Him to love you less. He's felt the same things, too, you know.

Crawl out of the pit and get going. Not sure what to do? Here are some ideas:
- Read a book.
- Browse through a bookstore.
- Start a journal.
- Write a poem.
- Paint a picture.
- Treat yourself to a movie.
- Organize your photos.
- Go jogging or work out.
- Make a new friend.

Embrace your circumstances. The truth is, it's OK to be alone from time to time. You might even come to enjoy time to yourself. There's a lot that can be accomplished when you're alone. Two of the most important things you can do alone are prayer and devotions. Group devotions and group prayer are vital, but it's just as important to spend some one-on-one time with God.

Sometimes being alone isn't your first choice, but it might be a blessing in disguise. Life will never slow down—cherish a little alone time when you can get it.

God Understands: A Sure-Fire Scripture Prescription

The Bible is filled with stories of desperately lonely people. Check out (and even consider memorizing) the following encouraging passages:

He who dwells in the shelter of the Most High will rest in the shadow of the Almighty.

I will say of the LORD, "He is my refuge and my fortress, my God, in whom I trust."

Surely he will save you from the fowler's snare and from the deadly pestilence.

He will cover you with his feathers, and under his wings you will find refuge; his faithfulness will be your shield and rampart.

—Ps. 91:1-4

Then I heard the voice of the Lord saying, "Whom shall I send? And who will go for us?"

And I said, "Here am I. Send me!"

—Isa. 6:8

Once you were alienated from God and were enemies in your minds because of your evil behavior. But now he has reconciled you by Christ's physical body through death to present you holy in his sight, without blemish and free from accusation—if you continue in your faith, established and firm, not moved from the hope held out in the gospel. This is the gospel that you heard and that has been proclaimed to every creature under heaven, and of which I, Paul, have become a servant.

—Col. 1:21-23

$$\boxed{7}$$

Money Matters

People who want to get rich fall into temptation and a trap and into many foolish and harmful desires that plunge men into ruin and destruction.
—1 Tim. 6:9

Maybe you're rich. Maybe you have a seven-digit account balance in a Swiss bank. Maybe you just sold the rights to your autobiography for a cool million. Maybe you don't even have to consider a part-time job this year to help your parents pay your tuition.

Yeah, right!

If you're like most everybody else, you'd be happy just to have a savings account. And chances are, you don't even have that—which makes launching out into the world kind of freaky right now.

Up to now, you've been the envy of the adult world—no need to pay rent, insurance, utilities, or car payments. But that all changes at graduation. Your freedom with money—and freedom from it—ends the second you walk across the platform and pick up that hard-earned high school diploma.

Don't panic. You're in the same shoes as most high school graduates. You can get the knack of handling your own finances just like thousands and thousands of others before you have. Here are some practical money-management tips to get you started in the world of finances, as well as some biblical advice that will help you get on the right track.

Delayed Gratification = Financial Maturity

Fact: You have limited resources and unlimited choices every day. The only way to survive financially is to exercise serious self-control. You must (1) deny yourself some of the things you would really like to have, (2) spend less money than you have coming in, and (3) avoid bad debts—such as carrying high credit card balances.

This simple plan for successful living can be summed up in this verse: "Keep your lives free from the love of money and be content with what you have" (Heb. 13:5).

Manage Your Money

ATMs are everywhere. They seem kind of like an unlimited well of the green stuff, a shining beacon that lights your path to spending nirvana. Just press a few buttons and, *voila!* cash appears. But sooner or later, if the amount coming out exceeds the amount going in—"Transaction Denied."

Don't fall into the economic abyss of maxed-out credit cards and overdrawn checking accounts. Set into motion now the discipline of managing your money.

• **Track your expenses with a simple budget.** At the top of a sheet of paper make a heading for each month starting with January. On the left-hand side, make a category titled "INCOME" (which lists all monthly sources of money) and a category titled "EXPENSES" (which lists all monthly bills). At the bottom add a category "AMOUNT LEFT OVER" (this is income minus expenses). With this type of simple budget you'll be able to look through the year and monitor your income, expenses, and savings.

• **Use credit cards cautiously.** View a credit card as another kind of checking account. Be absolutely sure that money is available to pay the bill in full when it comes due at the end of the month.

• **Get a clue about compound interest.** Understand that interest can work for you or against you. Compound interest requires that you pay back the amount you borrowed plus interest—and you pay back interest on interest! In other words, a $200 loan (such as the kind offered through a credit card) could end up costing you $300 to $400 to pay back as the interest on interest accumulates over the years. So how can compound interest work *for* you? Check out the next section for some ideas.

Invest in Things That Go Up

It sounds obvious, but a lot of people don't get this: Every time you spend money, you're making an investment; and what you invest in goes either up or down in value. The moment you buy a new shirt or stereo or movie rental or fast-food meal, you're money is gone. That's because you can never sell these things for as much as you paid for them. These are all "down" investments. But if you put that $5 or $10 or $50 in the bank, you could get it back with interest. Savings accounts are good "up" investments.

Tips for Compulsive Spenders

Ask why. Before you fork over cash, ask yourself, *Why do I want this?* If you can't come up with a good reason, put it back.

Count to seven. Live by the "seven-over-seven" rule. Anytime you want to spend more than $7 on something, wait seven days for it. This cooling-off period will help you decide whether you *really* want or need it.

Don't save by spending. Walk away when someone says a deal is too good to pass up or you'll never find as good a deal again. You'll always find as good a deal—sometimes even a better one. Even if the deal is incredible, investing in an "up" is an even better one. When the register tape at a discount store tells you that you've just saved $3 by shopping there, remind yourself that you haven't really saved anything—you've just spent $15.

Write it down. Every time you spend money on something, write it down. Just the trouble of recording the purchase will remind you of how much money waves goodbye to you for silly things. This is aversion therapy, the same as when your parents attempt to alter your behavior by making you write a hundred times, "I will not pin my little sister's doll collection to the ceiling. I will not pin my little sister's doll collection to the ceiling...."

Keep it at home. Figure out exactly how much money you'll need at the beginning of each day, and put that much in your wallet. Leave the rest of it at home.

8

51-and-a-Half Can't-Miss Practical Tips

Listen to advice and accept instruction,
and in the end you will be wise.
—Prov. 19:20

Auto Essentials

• Change the oil in your car every 3,000 miles.

• Keep jumper cables in your trunk. Even if you don't need them very often—a pair of jumper cables may allow you to be someone else's hero.

• Buy a local map.

• Frequently check the air pressure in your tires

• Have an emergency cell phone (or portable CB radio) in your car with a charger that plugs into your cigarette lighter).

• Keep an extra jug of window washer fluid in the trunk. If you don't, you'll surely run out when you need it the most. Trust us on this one.

• Keep a survival kit in your trunk. Pack it with a water bottle, blankets, dry food, flashlight, warm clothes, and so on.

Entertainment Ideas

• Find a friend and get lost together! Go somewhere you've never been before. Explore. Board a bus for an unknown destination. (Do this early in the day so you won't end up sleeping in the terminal.)

• Take a break with a silly television show or a favorite movie. Maybe even try a vintage black-and-white flick that you've never seen.

Faith Helps

• Memorize the words to your favorite praise song.

• Buy a great devotional book. It's handy to pull out a small but engaging devo book when you're standing in line, waiting for a bus, find yourself alone for a meal, and so on.

• Write a letter home to your family. Even though you may speak with them on the phone every week, it means a lot to them that you would take the time to *write* a letter or post card. Also, it's a good way to stay grounded spiritually—that is, if you're transparent enough to share prayer requests, struggles, even praises.

• Find someone back home who will be your "long-distance accountability partner." (If you end up staying in the same town, then find a guy or girl who will be your "phone accountability partner.") Vow to talk with this person at least once a week or no less than once a month. When you chat, share everything: prayer requests, struggles, praises, hopes, fears—even mundane, everyday kind of stuff.

Health Hints

• Exercise (walk, jog, ride a bicycle, play tennis). Even a little will help relieve a large amount of stress.

• Floss every day.

• Join a health club and set some goals: trimming down, building your biceps, increasing your endurance. By working out and getting some exercise on a daily basis, you can strengthen your body. And when you look your best, you feel good too.

Enjoying Your Castle

• Shop yard sales and flea markets for furniture, lamps, and other odds and ends for your first apartment.

• Buy cups, plates, utensils, toilet paper, light bulbs, and so on at your local discount dollar store.

• Use no-wipe shower spray in your tub after each use. This five-second task each day will help you avoid several hours of scrubbing soap scum from your grout.

• Take lots of photos. Take them of everyday occasions, not just special events.

Nutrition Nuts-n-Bolts

• Don't buy fresh food if you don't plan to eat it within two days.

• The most important meals of the day are breakfast and lunch. If you want energy during the day, don't skimp or eat on the run. And two bowls of cereal won't provide the balance you need to start the day. Try juice, a muffin, and some fruit or yogurt too.

• Take vitamin supplements only if you're certain you're not getting enough of one or more vitamins. If you're an athlete, keep in mind that consistent exercise (especially if you're training for a certain sport) results in increased activity, which will likely increase your food intake. This nearly always allows you to get the necessary vitamins your body needs to stay healthy.

Relocation Realities

• If you're apartment hunting, get one with an automatic dishwasher if at all possible. (You'll thank us later for this advice!)

• Before signing an apartment lease, read all the fine print first. Remember: a lease is a legal contract between you and the landlord. If you're the one entering into this binding agreement, you're the one liable for everything spelled out on the lease.

• If you choose to go to college and live on campus,

keep in mind that you'll probably have to pay as much as $200 for phone installation (flipping a switch) and service, room connection fees for Internet service, as well as a post office box rental fee.

Romance Starters—For Guys Only

• Score an A+ in the romance department. Buy your special lady one item from each of these stores: Crabtree & Evelyn, Hallmark Card Shop, a local flower shop, a top-quality jewelry store. For extra credit, have your surprises custom gift-wrapped.

• On Valentine's Day write "I love you" in seven different languages: *Je t'aime* (French), *Ti amo* (Italian), *Ai shite imasu* (Japanese), *Nagligivaget* (Eskimo), *Aloha wau ia oe* (Hawaiian), *S'agapo* (Greek), *Te amo* (Spanish).

• Treat her to a romantic movie marathon. You can include contemporary romantic comedies and some of the heavier dramas.

Romance Starters—For Gals Only

• Refill his box of Honeycombs with green M & M's. Also, place a photo of yourself inside the box.

• Each day this week, place one of the following items under his windshield wiper: a syrupy love note, a coupon to his favorite pizza place, a one-pound-size Hershey bar, a Starbuck's gift certificate, a card with Scripture verses handwritten inside, a promissory note good for one free shoulder rub, a single red rose.

• Have a photo of the two of you blown up to poster size. Place it in his dorm room or apartment when he's not home.

Study Strategies

• If you're having a hard time taking decent notes during class, ask your professor if you can audiotape the lectures.

• Don't procrastinate. Try this novel thought: Actually do assignments (reading chapters, writing papers) as they're assigned.

• Take a class just for personal enjoyment—such as cooking, photography, auto mechanics, fencing, surfing, painting, and so on.

Survival Smarts

• Always carry your I.D. with you—driver's license, school I.D., passport, and so on.

• Keep a first-aid kit in your dorm or apartment as well as in your car.

• Stock up on stuff like antacid tablets, aspirin, throat lozenges, stomach medicine, headache reliever, tissues, and so on. In other words, keep it stocked with anything you'll need in the middle of the night—you know, those miserable hours when you don't want to get dressed and make a trip to the pharmacy.

• Don't get trapped in quicksand. If you find yourself in this precarious predicament (as if that will happen), here's what you must do: Spread your arms and legs apart and attempt to float on your back. Next, position a large pole under your hips and at right angles to your spine. (When in quicksand country, it's always best to carry a pole with you!) Finally, keeping your hips afloat, *slowly* make your way to firmer ground.

• Never give anyone you *don't* know a ride—regardless of how cute he or she is.

• If your car breaks down and you have to walk to get help or make a phone call—never accept a ride from a stranger. This may seem like common sense, but in 110-degree weather five miles from the nearest exit, a ride might seem inviting. Bottom line: Don't do it. Walk.

• Avoid getting lost in the woods. Take some clues from the Boy Scouts: Never stray off a trail; tell someone where you're hiking, or better yet, hike *with* someone. Always carry a map, a whistle, a pack of matches or a lighter, a water bottle, a couple of Power Bars, and a mini-flashlight.

Tips from the "Duh" Files

- Always tip the pizza delivery guy.
- Never put anything metal in the microwave.
- Change your underwear every day.
- Call home at least once a week.
- Keep a list of people you lend your stuff to. (You know—things like books, CDs, DVDs, clothes, money.)

Travel Tidbits

- Pick your favorite airline, and sign up for its frequent flyer program. You can accrue miles for everything from flying, renting a car, using a credit card, staying at select hotels, ordering flowers, and more. Who knows? One day you may have enough points to take a free trip.

- Take a friend home with you during a long weekend. It's fun to introduce someone from your new world to the familiar places of your old life.

- Get bumped from a flight sometime when you're not in a hurry to get someplace. Why? You could end up with a voucher for a free flight, a possible upgrade (usually from coach to business class), a free stay in a hotel, and a free meal. Your chances of getting bumped are strongest if you choose a popular route that's traveled during a high-demand time such as Thanksgiving and Christmas.

Oh, and here's the "one-half tip": Share this book with a friend!

Part 3

Life-Changing Choices

9

Having Fun and Living to Tell About It

Be self-controlled and alert. Your enemy the devil prowls around like a roaring lion looking for someone to devour.
—1 Pet. 5:8

Sun. Sand. Surf. A dreamy stretch of Florida beach is exactly what Jeff had in mind for this year's spring break bash. So why is he sitting in the back of a police car instead of riding the waves?

"The guys and I got caught drinking in public," the embarrassed 18-year-old tells his parents later. "I can't believe we did it—we're all Christians. I should have said no when they handed me the first beer. I guess I got caught up in the moment and just wasn't thinking straight."

Nineteen-year-old Mandy is frustrated. What she thought would be a "girl's only" night of junk food and old movies with her two roommates suddenly went coed.

"Why can't you chill out like the rest of us?" whispers Terra, who's sharing an apartment with Mandy. Terra pops the top on a bottle of beer, peeks through the kitchen doors at the guys kicking back in her living room, and then glances back at Mandy. "So we're making the evening a little more interesting. It's OK—we're all grown-ups here. Besides, it wouldn't hurt you to loosen up a little!"

Does MasterCard Accept VISA?

Mandy rolls her eyes. "Give me a break! It's *not* OK! Every Saturday night turns into the same thing: a guy-chasing drinking fest. And to top it off, it usually becomes a sleepover."

Mandy grabs her jacket and storms out the front door. *I just can't deal with this anymore,* she tells herself. *What happened to my so-called Christian roommates? It's like they left their faith back in high school.*

Newfound Freedom

Once you're on your own, will you leave your faith back in high school too? Or will you strive to become the solid person God calls you to be? Will you fill the days ahead with authentic Christ-centered fun—and live to tell about it? Or will you slide toward what the world calls a good time and risk a life of regret?

As Jeff and Mandy discovered, being on your own is both a blessing and a curse.

The Blessing: *Independence!* Those clashes with pesky siblings, constant 10 P.M. curfews, and endless "Not-while-you're-living-under-my-roof" lectures become nothing more than murky adolescent memories.

The Curse: *Independence!* Your parents, siblings, and youth minister aren't there to bail you out if you get into trouble. The support system you once depended on is now gone—or at least in a different state.

The fact is, you—and only you—will be responsible for your actions. Making the right choices and dealing with the wrong ones are things you'll have to shoulder all by yourself. So will you choose to bend the rules from time to time just because you can, or will you commit to an unshakable faith in Christ?

Now is the time to decide. Like it or not, the days ahead will be filled with all kinds of temptations. And get this: the pressure won't always come from your peers.

Case in point: During my sophomore year of college I (Michael) was offered illegal drugs by a most unlikely source—one of my college professors. While attending a secular university in northern California, I joined one of my graphic design classes on a field trip to a major advertising agency in San Francisco. It was roughly a six-hour drive from the college campus. Many of the students drove their own cars, but about six of us piled into the back of our professor's pick-up truck. He had a canopy on the back, which meant we were slightly cramped, yet cozy!

It was an exciting trip; my new friends and I laughed and told stories in the back of the truck. Suddenly our professor slid open the cab window and handed back some sort of pipe with something burning in it. The odor was sweet and weird, and I wasn't sure what it was. Our teacher exclaimed, "This will make the trip go by faster!"

One of my fellow students looked at the pipe with a puzzled expression, then said, "Pot? Our professor's doin' drugs!"

Without hesitation, he handed the pipe to me. I winced and passed it to the next student. "No, thanks, " I said, "I don't do drugs."

The pipe made its way around the entire group without anyone taking a hit. One of the girls handed the pipe back to our professor.

Slightly confused and, perhaps, a little bit high, our instructor stuck his head through the window and scowled. "What's the matter with you? You're college students! Don't any of you know how to party?"

Surviving the Social Scene

I'm thankful that I didn't cave in and end up as a bad witness. Yet I have friends who for one reason or another left their faith in high school, making their newfound freedom a rough, sad, and downright *ugly* experience.

It doesn't have to be that way. Whether you've just headed into your senior year of high school or have already graduated, there's a lot you can do to make sure your foundation in Christ is strong enough to withstand any temptation you encounter. Take the following faith steps.

Faith step No. 1: Get connected

Right now is the perfect time to grow closer to Jesus and to lay a foundation for Him to build on when you go off to college or out on your own. Why? Because you have a support system to plug into: family, church, friends. Train hard now so that when the time comes to head off on your own, you'll have the resolve to continue following God consistently and fervently. He not only wants you to survive but also plans for you to *thrive* in your new life ahead.

Faith step No. 2: Focus your identity

A lot of teenagers spend considerable energy trying to figure out their personalities, style, and peer group during high school. The truth is, it's not too different out in the real world. It just gets more complicated. As guys and girls test their new freedom, often with some downright wild and crazy behavior, they sometimes lose sight of who they really are deep down inside.

Guess what—you don't have to get lost in the crowd. Check out 2 Cor. 5:17: "If anyone is in Christ, he is a new creation; the old has gone, the new has come!" A new creation—that was the starting point! Why bother being "the old" when "the new" has come? The Lord will keep you on track by helping you regain a sense of your identity in Him.

Faith step No. 3: Write yourself a letter

Here's a step you can take to save some pain during your first year out on your own. Set aside some time very soon to write yourself a letter. Write out what being a Christian means to you, explaining how being a new creation affects your behavior and choices as well as describing the kind of person Christ wants you to be. Don't forget to list your core Christian values somewhere in your letter. Next, put the note in an envelope labeled "Open on my first day of college (military post, new job, or so on)." You'll thank yourself later for taking this step.

Rescue 911: The Truth About Sex, Drug Abuse, and Drinking

We get hundreds of letters from teens and college students with questions on nearly every topic imaginable. Here are some questions we've received and answers we've given about sex, drugs, and drinking.

"What's Wrong with Using Sex as Recreation?"

Q. Why make such a big deal out of something that's so natural? If two unmarried people agree to have sex with each other, why label it a sin? Can't sex be another form of recreation?

A. True, sex is great in the right setting—marriage. Why label it as "sinful" if it happens outside of holy matrimony? Because that's what the Bible calls it. See Exod. 20:14; Matt. 5:27-30; 1 Cor. 6:15-20; 7:2, 9; and 1 Thess. 4:3-8.

Why make such a big deal out of sex? Because it *is* a big deal. Unlike anything else a married couple may experience, sexual intercourse creates the deepest, most powerful bond—sort of a relational Super Glue. And that bond is never supposed to be broken. *Sex isn't just physical,* and it's not a trivial act that feels good for a few seconds and then is over for good. For a couple, sex involves the body, mind, and emotions in an activity that is *intended to be shared for a lifetime.*

Unlike dogs, cats, and other members of the animal kingdom who are slaves to their instincts, humans are given free choice and self-control. God expects us—and helps us—to control our desires and to wait for His timing and His best plans for us.

"Why Are Pot and Other Illegal Drugs Off Limits?"

Q. A lot of people my age smoke pot. I've tried it, and—I won't lie—I liked it. Is it really wrong for Christians to use this and other illegal drugs? Didn't God say in Genesis to live off the seeds of the earth?

A. We assume you're talking about Gen. 1:29. That's where God says, "I give you every seed-bearing plant on the face of the whole earth and every tree that has fruit with seed in it." If this is the passage you're referring to, then why leave off the last part of the verse? In it God says, "They will be yours for food." (Not for smoking!)

There's a whole lot more we could write about this issue—such as how pot and other drugs can be harmful to your life emotionally, physically, and spiritually. But there might be a simpler way. Just use the list below to see if using pot or any other drug is OK for you as a Christian.

• It will cause me to disobey the law.

• It will cause me to disobey my parents as well as other people who have authority over my life.

• It may cause me to lie.

• It may be harmful to my physical body. (See 1 Cor. 6:19-20.)

• It can potentially have the same effect on my judgment and behavior as drunkenness.

If you checked one or more of these statements, then you have your answer: Smoking pot or using any other illegal drug is a sin.

Here's a four-point strategy for staying drug-free:

1. Get the facts straight. "I'll try it just once—it can't hurt, and I won't turn into a druggie." This is the lie of the century. Don't be fooled—illegal drugs kill. A "high" may feel good for a little while, but the drug is poisoning your body. Take in too much of it, or keep using it, and your body breaks down and dies.

2. Don't even get started. The best defense against illegal drugs is to avoid them. Don't give in—even once.

3. Seek help. If you have a friend who is in trouble, you've got to do more than just watch. Talk to a parent or a teacher. If you think he or she wouldn't get the picture, go to a coach, a counselor, or your minister.

4. Make a pact with God. The Holy Spirit gives us the wisdom to make good decisions along with the strength to carry them out. The fact is, we serve a God with guts— a God who is strong and courageous.

"What Does the Bible Say About Drinking?"

Q. Several months ago I tried alcohol for the first time with a couple of friends. Since then, I've been tempted to drink again. What does the Bible say about alcohol?

A. It says a lot. Here are some highlights:

1. Drunkenness is completely off-limits. See Eph. 5:18.

2. Adults are permitted to drink a little wine for health reasons (see 1 Tim. 5:23). Yet in Num. 6:3 God instructed those who wanted to make a special vow to "abstain from wine and other fermented drink."

3. Rom. 14:14-21 tells us to avoid doing anything that might cause another person to stumble. So if you openly kick back with a beer, you're telling others that it's OK to drink. But your attitude shouldn't be, *Hey—this doesn't hurt me, so what's the big deal?* You need to ask, *How will this affect my friends?*

4. First Cor. 6:12 says, "'Everything is permissible for me'—but not everything is beneficial. 'Everything is per-

missible for me'—but I will not be mastered by anything."

In other words, it's not a question of "Can I drink?" It's an issue of "Should I?" Those who are wise don't see how close they can get to the edge without sinning. Rather, they tell themselves, *If I never take the very first drink, then I don't have to worry about ever getting drunk or hurting myself and others.*

Having said all this, I remind you of what the Bible says regarding three other simple matters:

- **Lying to authority figures:** Don't do it.

Is drinking with your friends something you would hide from the authority figures in your life?

- **Disobeying parents:** Don't do it.

If you're not yet 21, have your parents given you their blessing regarding the illegal use of alcohol?

- **Disobeying the civil laws:** Don't do it.

If you're under the legal drinking age and still choose to drink, then you're breaking the law. Check out Rom. 13:1-7 for more on this subject.

10

The Church Search

Choosing Wisely and Plugging In

See to it that no one takes you captive through hollow and deceptive philosophy, which depends on human tradition and the basic principles of this world rather than on Christ.
—Col. 2:8

Let's be honest: even some of the most committed Christians are tempted to spend their Sunday mornings snoozing in the toasty comfort of First Church of the Warm Bed. And the temptation only gets worse when you're on your own. Especially if your roommate is a committed member of Bedside Baptist.

Without sending you on a guilt trip, we want to emphasize two of the most important steps you'll take when you leave home: Regardless of where you end up, find a solid, Bible-believing church, and plug in right away.

Why Plugging In Is So Important

1. There's no such thing as a Lone Ranger Christian. Worshiping God is an interactive experience. It's meant to be shared with others. Even if it seems that your pastor is preaching in Greek or you couldn't find the Book of Micah if your life depended upon it, spending time in church teaches you that God's family is a whole lot bigger than your parents, sisters, and pesky little brother. Get this: Heaven is going to be packed with all kinds of people praising and worshiping God. Church is a good place to prepare. What's more, your church family keeps you accountable.

   2. **Going to church plugs you in to God's truth.** Face it: we encounter a lot of distractions during the week—in a college classroom, at work, on television, with our friends. Too many things can pull us away from God. Sunday mornings give us a spiritual zap—and get us back on track.

   3. **Church gives you a chance to be fed from God's Word.** Now, you might say, "But I can do that by reading the Bible; can't I have a day off?" And we would ask, what if the cafeteria staff on your college campus used that approach in preparing meals? "We feed you six days every week. Why don't you take a day off from eating?" OK, lousy example. Skipping a meal from the cafeteria might not be a bad idea—but you get the idea! Getting a daily, balanced diet is probably important to you. Getting a solid spiritual diet should be equally important.

Why the Church Search Is So Important

   I (Tiffany) was beginning to get impatient. Finding the right church was no easy task, and the same questions kept swirling through my head: *How do I find the right place to worship? Is there some sort of "spiritual checklist" I should be following? What if I pick the wrong church? I've been praying for months now—am I somehow just not getting through to God?*

   It was my first semester of college, a Christian college where I found myself connecting with dozens of other people my age. For the first month or two, finding a place to worship was a no-brainer: I merely followed everyone else to a megachurch that was associated with our school. (Hey, it had the added benefit of being close to campus.)

   Our college Sunday School class was jam-packed, and the teachers even had to use microphones in order to be heard. At first I was pretty amazed: There were skits, games, prizes, videos, and guest speakers. It was way different from my tiny church back home.

But after a few weeks had raced by, the class began to shrink both in class size and appeal. I learned that many of my fellow students were checking out other churches.

Why would they do that? I asked myself. After all, considering the small town where I grew up, I wasn't used to choices. I had just assumed that once I found a church that matched my doctrinal mind-set, it would be the one for me. But as a few more weeks went by, I began to realize the mistake I had made: When faced with the choice between several exceptional churches in my new college town, I had simply floated to the closest (and safest) one.

Before long, yet another mistake dawned on me: I had never prayed about this all-important decision of finding the right church family. So I did some soul-searching and began asking God some serious questions: *What's Your will, Lord? Have I settled into the right place? Is there another church You would like me to visit? Is this exhausting church search really that important?*

Once I prayed diligently and consistently for guidance, God began to speak quietly, showing me that I needed to take a risk, get out of my comfort zone, and connect with another congregation in town. Yet I didn't know exactly which church He had in mind. This predicament really scared me.

I held tightly to my parents' advice—"Find a solid Bible-believing church, and get plugged in"—and I continued to pray.

Lord, I don't have a clue how to find the right church, but I'm trusting You. Lead me, guide me, and help me to be faithful.

During the Sundays that followed, I plunged into my church search by visiting many solid Christian congregations. Some were a bit stiff for my taste, and some catered to the—well, shall we say—"geriatric" crowd. A few were quite inspirational, while others were just plain boring. Through it all, I continued to ask God, *Please lead me—because I don't know what I'm doing.*

In the past I had heard preachers complain about how many people get lazy and pick the church they find most entertaining. So I couldn't help but wonder, *Is that what I'm doing?* I had also heard that some churches appear to be biblically sound on the surface yet teach their *own* twisted form of religion. These thoughts also scared me—so, again, I retreated to do what I was becoming pretty good at: I prayed.

Then it happened. One particular Sunday morning, several weeks into my search, I found my church home. Right away I felt the presence of the Holy Spirit.

The senior pastor delivered a sermon from the Old Testament that held my attention like no other message I had ever heard. And deep inside, Jesus began to embrace my soul. He also issued one more gentle warning: *You're not finished yet. There's more work to do!*

As I prayed, I sensed Christ telling me to find out more about the church. So I did. I read the congregation's newsletter, visited Sunday School classes, sought the advice of friends who had lived in town for several years, and continued to attend Sunday morning services.

Before I knew it, I received the long-awaited green light from God. And as I prayed about my decision, I began to feel true peace from the Lord.

I attended this church during the remainder of my college career. To this day, I can still remember so many spiritual lessons that I gained from this church family.

So back to my original question: *Is this exhausting church search really that important?* The answer is absolutely! And through this faith-stretching journey, I learned some vital lessons about prayer, dependence upon God, and obedience.

Don't snooze through Sunday mornings or settle for a mundane church experience. Get out of your comfort zone and get connected.

Key Questions to Ask

As you embark upon your own church search, here are a few key questions you should ask yourself:

- Have I prayed for guidance?
- How do I define a "good church"?
- Who do I know in town who could honestly give advice on a particular church?
- Am I looking simply for entertainment?
- Has God already led me to the correct church?
- Have I ever researched the doctrinal beliefs of my previous church?
- Would a different church more closely fit my core beliefs in God?
- How many churches have I visited?
- How many Sunday School classes have I visited?

Church-Finding Checklist

- Is its foundation based on the Bible?
- Is Jesus the head of the church?
- Does it teach that only God saves, heals, and restores?
- What is its stance on the Holy Trinity?
- Does it teach John 3:16, that God gave His only Son (Jesus) to die on the Cross for the sins of the world?
- Does it encourage all members to have a personal relationship with Christ through prayer, study, and obedience?
- Is it involved in missions?
- Does it equip its members to go out and proclaim the message of God?
- What type of church government oversees the integrity and structure of the church?

Does MasterCard Accept VISA?

• What is the background of the senior pastor and others on the staff?

• How will you connect with this church body—Sunday School, small groups, activities, times of fellowship?

• Does the worship (music and sermons) glorify God?

11

What's Your Worldview?

What is being?
—Aristotle

The soul is the mirror of an indestructible universe.
—Gottfried Wilhelm Leibniz

Truth can be denied, but it cannot be avoided.
—Author unknown

Why do precisely these objects which we behold make a world?
—Henry David Thoreau

Out of the crooked timber of humanity no straight thing can ever be made.
—Immanuel Kant

I tell you the truth, whoever hears my word and believes him who sent me has eternal life and will not be condemned; he has crossed over from death to life.
—Jesus Christ (John 5:24)

Remember who you are and what you believe.
—Your mother

Help!

I (Tiffany) knew that college would be a mind-stretching experience, but all these new ideas were beginning to melt my brain cells. My philosophy professor's lectures sounded more like the dialogue in a foreign film.

I was learning about concepts like "postmodernism" and "relativism." What are they? They're worldviews—

ways that people think and believe, that, in these cases, deny any ultimate truth or absolute right and wrong, especially if it has to do with God. These philosophies dominate much of today's culture. "Possibly even the mindset of your own," my professor warned.

My head was spinning. I was both confused and intrigued. I also knew that my only hope of surviving Philosophy 101 would be to join forces with other students. My solution: Plug into a study group (one that consisted of solid Christians). I had assumed that a pack of like-minded peers would offer a safe haven, an ideal environment in which to explore alien worldviews—and even to get an interpretation or two.

Unfortunately, my assumptions were wrong—way wrong!

The other students were just as confused as I was. And like me, most had more questions than answers. A bitter truth quickly set in: If I was going to stay afloat, I would have to swim hard and attempt to figure things out on my own. I would have to salvage those melting brain cells—*and actually think!*

Like Drinking from a Fire Hose

We were just a few weeks into the course when some of my peers seemed to check their brains at the door, numbing their senses and resolving to do the minimum to get by. (You know, memorizing a few names and dates in history along with some quotes from the so-called "great thinkers" of our time.) Despite feeling overwhelmed, that strategy just didn't cut it for me.

I wanted to do well. I knew I would have to step out of the box and attempt to grasp the larger concepts. Deep inside, I knew there was a lot more at stake than merely getting a passing grade. I was actually given an opportunity to examine my core beliefs—and then to grow deeper in my Christian walk.

In the days ahead, I found myself asking some serious

questions: *Who's right? Do these concepts contradict my belief in God? Is it good for me to study various views on life, or am I treading into dangerous territory? Why is it so hard to defend the omniscience of God in a class debate? If so many people struggle with these questions, why haven't I encountered them before?*

I felt my brain stretch with each new question.

Bottom line: Not only did I survive my philosophy class, but this and numerous other challenging experiences became defining moments in my life. God used them to strengthen and focus my Christian worldview. He literally shook my foundation and forced me to wrestle with the greater questions in life: *Who am I? Where do I fit in? What truly motivates me? Do my beliefs align with "the Alpha and the Omega . . . who is, and who was, and who is to come, the Almighty"* (Rev. 1:8)?

I questioned, I learned, and I walked away with a much deeper understanding and belief in Jesus Christ.

Whether you head off to college or the military or the workplace, don't just check your brains at the door and accept everything you're told. And certainly don't allow your faith to grow numb and mindless. I challenge you to *challenge everything!* Use your brain, think for yourself, explore the deep questions in life. Above all, ask God to open your eyes and ground you in truth—absolute truth.

But I must warn you: There's a fine balance between standing firm on your beliefs and exploring new ideas and concepts. So how do you keep from losing your balance (and the truth)? Keep reading.

Tuning In to Truth

Mind your motives. Ultimately, any true pursuit of God will lead to God, because there's only one truth. But as you explore philosophies and worldviews that differ from Christianity, be on guard. "See to it that no one takes you captive through hollow and deceptive philosophy, which depends on human tradition and the basic principles of this world rather than on Christ" (Col. 2:8). The key to staying grounded in God is to "check your pulse" from time to time. Clue into your motives by asking yourself some questions: *Am I trying to better understand God? Am I studying the beliefs of others in order to better understand human nature and their interpretations of God? Am I trying to disprove God in order to run from Him?* Question yourself.

Pray often. Pray hard! The best piece of advice I have received is actually pretty simple: *Pray!* Pray about everything. Talk to God about your confusion, your fears, and your desire to know the truth. Ask for wisdom. Ask for guidance. Ask for a true heart. Even when you're not sure what you believe—pray.

Study the Word. Too often in life, I find that my times with the Lord become rushed: I fly through a few verses and then say a quick prayer before heading out the door in the morning. But gradually and patiently, God is teaching me that the core things in life—especially my relationship with Him—can't be rushed. I need to slow down, disconnect from the world, and immerse myself in the truth. I need to savor God's Word daily.

So why is reading and studying the Bible so important? Because Scripture strengthens your *Christian mind.* That's right—the New Testament says to "be transformed by the renewing of your mind" (Rom. 12:2).

If you don't know what it's built on, how can you defend your faith when students and professors or people in the workplace don't take it seriously? Get excited, and get serious about saturating your mind with the wisdom of God and defending His truth before a world that denies it.

Find strength in numbers. "Two are better than one, because they have a good return for their work. If one falls down, his friend can help him up" (Eccles. 4:9-10). As you get into the habit of praying and spending time in God's Word every day, start asking Him for some great friendships with other Christians. Building a strong faith foundation, especially when you're out on your own, takes help from others. Seek friends who share your values—those who will sharpen you, encourage you, and help you grow and stand strong in the Lord.

Will you be ready when your faith foundation is challenged everywhere from the social scene to the classroom to the workplace?

Maintaining a Godly Worldview
Some Passages to Ponder

- Eph. 5:1-10
- Rom. 13:12-14
- James 4:1-10
- Heb. 13:5-6
- 1 John 2:15-17
- 1 John 2:20-27
- Prov. 23:19-23

12

Marriage or Singleness?

"I know the plans I have for you," declares the LORD, "plans to prosper you and not to harm you, plans to give you hope and a future."
—Jer. 29:11

One minute I (Michael) am surfing the tube, looking for something decent to watch, and the next minute I'm outraged. *What I'm seeing can't be real!* I tell myself. *It's got to be staged. Who actually lives this way?*

I've stumbled upon the "The Ricki Lake Show." Today's topic: "Transvestite Gay Men and Their Female Lovers."

Ricki is interviewing a gay man named Charlie who is dressed like a woman and a lady named Sarah who is dressed like a man. They claim to be lovers. Suddenly the woman pulls an engagement ring out of her jacket pocket and kneels in front of the man.

"Charlie, we've been friends for a long time," she says, "and you know how I feel about you."

The man blushes, and the audience starts cheering.

"I want to spend my life with you," Sarah tells Charlie, offering him the ring. "I want to have your children. That's why I'm asking you to marry me."

The audience roars even louder. Even Ricki begins to pressure him. "So what's your answer, Charlie?" Ricki says. "She obviously loves you. Are you going to say no to this beautiful lady?"

"But I'm gay," Charlie responds.

"I don't care," his lover says. "I think we can have a good life together."

Does MasterCard Accept VISA?

After a long pause, the audience still cheering, Charlie looks at Ricki and says, "Yes—I'll marry her. But only because I love that gorgeous ring!"

As outrageous as this scenario may seem, it speaks to me about the casual attitudes our culture holds toward marriage.

True, Charlie and Sarah represent an extreme case, certainly not the norm. Yet too many well-meaning couples—even Christian couples—move glibly through courtship and into marriage without fully grasping just how much is at stake for them. And some of the reasons they give for heading down the aisle are just as weak as the one Charlie came up with: "All my friends and family have tied the knot." "I don't want to be alone." "I'm a romantic at heart who loves being in a relationship." "My parents expect me to get married." "Everybody at church will think I'm abnormal if I remain single."

When it comes to matters of the heart, where do you stand? Do you desire to be married one day, or do you sense that God is calling you to a life of singleness?

If marriage is in your future, and if you're currently in a relationship, how can you be certain that the romantic love you're experiencing today is the kind that will last tomorrow—and all the tomorrows to come? More specifically, at what point can you be confident that the man or woman you're currently seeing is the person you should marry?

Choosing a lifetime mate is one of the biggest decisions you'll ever make, so you're wise to ponder these questions carefully and soberly. Above all, enter a romantic relationship with your eyes wide open, and bathe the whole experience in prayer. The fact is this—a bad marriage is much worse than not being married at all.

In the pages that follow, we'll explore this important

part of your life, and we'll zero in on some ways you can seek to protect your heart from major attack.

The Secret to Lifelong Love

If you're convinced that marriage is in your future, understand this: God doesn't expect you to search the earth for the "one-and-only" person He has in mind for you. (What are the chances of ever finding that person?) Instead, here's a promise He gives you: "I know the plans I have for you . . . plans to prosper you and not to harm you, plans to give you hope and a future" (Jer. 29:11).

When it comes to relationships, the Lord is instructing us to walk by faith. He also wants us to use our heads and to take the following careful steps:

Ask some tough questions.

• What qualities are important in the man or woman I marry?

• Does he or she love Jesus?

• Does he or she share some of my dreams and life goals?

• Do I enjoy his or her company?

Clue into what lasting love is all about.

"Love"—it's probably the most overused word in the English language. You might say: "I love Dad and Mom," "I love pepperoni pizza," "I love being alone," "I love that special person I'm dating," "I love God."

"Love" means something different in each case.

In the Bible, the word often refers to action—something we do rather than something we *feel.* John 3:16 says, "God so loved the world that he gave . . ." This verse refers to love as an action, something God *did* for us. In other places throughout Scripture, love is defined as selfless giving to others, of manifesting attitudes of kindness, patience, humility, and commitment in relationships.

So what does love as an action have to do with the warm, fuzzy, head-over-heels kind we experience in romantic relationships? Everything.

Does MasterCard Accept VISA?

The kind of love we share with our marriage partner goes way beyond simple emotions. This kind of love involves commitment. It means putting the needs of another above your own: "It is not rude, it is not self-seeking, it is not easily angered, it keeps no record of wrongs. Love does not delight in evil but rejoices with the truth" (1 Cor. 13:5-6).

Avoid being "unequally yoked."

Let's go straight to the Bible for some direction regarding this issue. Take a look at 2 Cor. 6:14-15. It says, "Do not be yoked together with unbelievers. For what do righteousness and wickedness have in common? Or what fellowship can light have with darkness? . . . What does a believer have in common with an unbeliever?" These are good questions to ask yourself.

The fact is, when two people are yoked together, they must both pull in the same direction. But by definition, Christians and non-Christians are headed in different directions. Apply this to romance, and you have disaster. The couple ends up going nowhere, and they keep rubbing the sores on each other in the process. Getting involved romantically just won't work.

The Blessing of Marriage

The day I asked Tiffany to marry me was certainly a defining moment in my life—an eternal snapshot, so to speak—that represented the beginning of an awesome journey as well as the culmination of thousands of moments Tiffany and I had already spent together.

It was Christmas Eve 1996, and Tiffany and I had spent the afternoon hiking in the wilderness near her parents' home in Pineville, West Virginia.

"This is my favorite spot," Tiffany said when we reached the end of the trail, a steep ridge with a postcard-perfect view. "I used to come here when I had big decisions to make."

"I can see why," I said. "This place definitely feels a little closer to God."

Rugged mountains and misty groves of oak and spruce stretched endlessly across the West Virginia landscape. It didn't take a bolt of lightning to convince me that the setting was ideal, and the moment was right. More important, I knew that Tiffany was the right woman.

Asking this incredible lady to spend her life with me involved a risk. After all, God could have had other plans for her. Yet several key things had given me confidence:

Tiffany and I had built our relationship on a foundation of . . .

Faith. Jesus and His will for our lives are the center of our desires. He defines our self-worth, not the status of being in a relationship.

Friendship. We had spent a little more than two years getting to know each other. This meant countless hours having fun together and asking each other hard questions. True intimacy always grows slowly out of the solid soil of "knowing" each other casually and intently.

Support. We kept our relationship within sight of our families. One of the first steps I took was to ask Tiffany's dad for his permission to marry his daughter as well as his blessing on our life together.

Purity. Nothing can ruin a relationship more quickly than going too far too fast too soon. I'm proud we made a commitment to stay pure for each other and for God.

As Tiffany and I stood there on that ridge soaking in the beauty of our surroundings, I reached into my jacket pocket and pulled out a small velvet box. I handed it to Tiffany and smiled. "I have an early Christmas gift for you," I said.

She ran her finger across the lid and smiled back. "I bet it's jewelry!"

As Tiffany reached in and gently pulled out a diamond engagement ring, the expression on her face gave me a solid clue to her answer.

I knelt. "I couldn't imagine spending the rest of this life without you," I said, looking into her eyes. "Will you marry me?"

Tiffany's smile grew even bigger. "Yes!"

Before we headed down the mountain to share the news with Tiffany's family, I spent some time talking to my Father: *Thank you, God, for this priceless woman you've given me. Waiting for her has been worth it. I give You this marriage. Bless it, use it, and let Your will be done.*

The Gift of Singleness

When you think about the gifts of the Holy Spirit, what kinds of things come to mind? Wisdom from the Lord? Serving others? Showing mercy? Teaching?

Consider yet another: singleness. That's right. The apostle Paul calls singleness a gift from God: "I wish that all men were as I am. But each man has his own gift from God; one has this gift, another has that" (1 Cor. 7:7). And Paul was determined to use this special gift as a way to serve and encourage other Christians. Because he did not have a wife, he knew he could devote himself wholeheartedly to ministry.

C. S. Lewis, who spent most of his life as a bachelor, had an interesting perspective on this subject. In his book *Letters to an American Lady* (1962, 109-10), he says this about the issue of marriage versus singleness:

I nominally have (a place of my own) and am nominally master of the house, but things seldom go as I would have chosen. The truth is that the only alternatives are either solitude (with all its miseries and dangers, both moral and physical) or else all the rubs and frustrations of a joint life. The second, even at its worst seems to me far the better. . . . We are *all* fallen creatures and *all* very hard to live with.

Consider this: Singleness can be good. It was for Paul, and for that matter, it was right for Jesus. If this is what God wants for your life, then He'll make it a right and good experience. And get this: the Bible never talks about singleness as being second-rate. It need not be unfulfilled. It need not be unhappy.

One of the worst things you can do as a single person is to believe the lie that you're second-rate because you're not yet married—or that you're living your life in limbo, always waiting for someone to come along. If God has truly given you the gift of singleness, be thankful, and enjoy this gift to the fullest.

Conclusion
Wise Words for Every Need

Your word is a lamp to my feet and a light for my path.
—Ps. 119:105

Ready to launch your dreams? Ready for the real world?

Regardless of what you achieve and where your feet take you in life, we urge you to carry the ultimate lantern, the one-and-only lamp that can keep each step you take firmly planted in the light of Christ. We're talking, of course, about the Holy Bible. "All Scripture is God-breathed and is useful for teaching, rebuking, correcting and training in righteousness, so that the man of God may be thoroughly equipped for every good work" (2 Tim. 3:16-17).

By now you've figured out that the purpose of this book is to offer some encouragement and practical tips that will help you get where you want to be in life—especially on a path that leads to eternal life through Jesus. We can't think of a better way to end our time together than to refocus our eyes on the Bible.

On the pages that follow, we'll explore some timeless wisdom and eternal promises from the Scriptures. As you read, you'll discover that God's Word offers guidance for just about every situation you'll ever encounter.

Wise Advice When You Feel . . .

Angry

A patient man has great understanding, but a quick-tempered man displays folly (Prov. 14:29).

Does MasterCard Accept VISA?

"In your anger do not sin": Do not let the sun go down while you are still angry, and do not give the devil a foothold (Eph. 4:26-27).

Anxious

Do not be anxious about anything, but in everything, by prayer and petition, with thanksgiving, present your requests to God. And the peace of God, which transcends all understanding, will guard your hearts and your minds in Christ Jesus (Phil. 4:6-7).

Cast all your anxiety on him because he cares for you (1 Pet. 5:7).

Brokenhearted

Even though I walk through the valley of the shadow of death, I will fear no evil, for you are with me; your rod and your staff, they comfort me (Ps. 23:4).

He heals the brokenhearted and binds up their wounds (Ps. 147:3).

Confused

Trust in the LORD with all your heart and lean not on your own understanding; in all your ways acknowledge him, and he will make your paths straight (Prov. 3:5-6).

Where you have envy and selfish ambition, there you find disorder and every evil practice (James 3:16).

Depressed

Fear not, for I have redeemed you; I have summoned you by name; you are mine. When you pass through the waters, I will be with you; and when you pass through the rivers, they will not sweep over you. When you walk through the fire, you will not be burned; the flames will not set you ablaze (Isa. 43:1-2).

Peace I leave with you; my peace I give you. I do not

give to you as the world gives. Do not let your hearts be troubled and do not be afraid (John 14:27).

Discouraged

Though I walk in the midst of trouble, you preserve my life; you stretch out your hand against the anger of my foes, with your right hand you save me (Ps. 138:7).

The ransomed of the LORD will return. They will enter Zion with singing; everlasting joy will crown their heads. Gladness and joy will overtake them, and sorrow and sighing will flee away (Isa. 51:11).

Fearful

The LORD is my light and my salvation—whom shall I fear? The LORD is the stronghold of my life—of whom shall I be afraid? When evil men advance against me to devour my flesh, when my enemies and my foes attack me, they will stumble and fall. Though an army besiege me, my heart will not fear; though war break out against me, even then will I be confident. One thing I ask of the LORD, this is what I seek: that I may dwell in the house of the LORD all the days of my life, to gaze upon the beauty of the LORD and to seek him in his temple (Ps. 27:1-4).

Inferior

You created my inmost being; you knit me together in my mother's womb. I praise you because I am fearfully and wonderfully made; your works are wonderful, I know that full well. My frame was not hidden from you when I was made in the secret place. When I was woven together in the depths of the earth, your eyes saw my unformed body. All the days ordained for me were written in your book before one of them came to be (Ps. 139:13-16).

We are God's workmanship, created in Christ Jesus to do good works, which God prepared in advance for us to do (Eph. 2:10).

Does MasterCard Accept VISA?

Lonely

Who shall separate us from the love of Christ? Shall trouble or hardship or persecution or famine or nakedness or danger or sword? As it is written: "For your sake we face death all day long; we are considered as sheep to be slaughtered." No, in all these things we are more than conquerors through him who loved us. For I am convinced that neither death nor life, neither angels nor demons, neither the present nor the future, nor any powers, neither height nor depth, nor anything else in all creation, will be able to separate us from the love of God that is in Christ Jesus our Lord (Rom. 8:35-39).

Rejected

For the sake of his great name the LORD will not reject his people, because the LORD was pleased to make you his own (1 Sam. 12:22).

I will not leave you as orphans; I will come to you (John 14:18).

Tempted

No temptation has seized you except what is common to man. And God is faithful; he will not let you be tempted beyond what you can bear. But when you are tempted, he will also provide a way out so that you can stand up under it (1 Cor. 10:13).

Because he himself suffered when he was tempted, he is able to help those who are being tempted (Heb. 2:18).

Unworthy

"Ah, Sovereign LORD," I said, "I do not know how to speak; I am only a child."

But the LORD said to me, "Do not say, 'I am only a child.' You must go to everyone I send you to and say whatever I command you. Do not be afraid of them, for I am with you and will rescue you," declares the LORD.

Conclusion

Then the Lord reached out his hand and touched my mouth and said to me, "Now, I have put my words in your mouth. See, today I appoint you over nations and kingdoms to uproot and tear down, to destroy and overthrow, to build and to plant" (Jer. 1:6-10).

Worried

Do not worry about your life, what you will eat or drink; or about your body, what you will wear. Is not life more important than food, and the body more important than clothes? Look at the birds of the air; they do not sow or reap or store away in barns, and yet your heavenly Father feeds them. Are you not much more valuable than they? Who of you by worrying can add a single hour to his life? (Matt. 6:25-27).